600 Fortnite Tricks

The Expanded Fortnite Battle Royale
Strategy Guide

Sam Chang

600 Fortnite Tricks

1. Always carry an SMG/AR so you can do chip damage from a safe distance.

2. Use compass directions to relay information to teammates. "North" is more accurate than "straight ahead."

3. If you're sieging an enemy's tower, try and focus on collapsing the entire thing. They'll fall and be vulnerable.

4. If you snipe someone in the body, he's gonna run and hide and you won't get another chance. Aim for the head!

5. If you're struggling with solo mode, try filling in for squads. You might learn some tricks from experienced players.

6. Make sure to add a delay to your stream if you're playing in a tournament. Don't get sniped!

7. Harvest materials as soon as you land at the start of the game. An early ramp can make all the difference.

8. Don't focus on the rarity color of weapons you find. Many blue guns are better than purple guns! Even some legendary weapons are trash.

9. Don't be afraid to abandon your fort if you're getting shot by multiple enemies. You can rebuild your fort, but you can't come back to life.

⍰

10. Always drop a ramp or defensive wall before shooting someone. Even if you're ambushing them from behind.

11. Bullets drop as they travel. So aim above your enemy's head if you want to a headshot with the bolt-action.

12. Find a Fortnite group at school/work and talk strategies during downtime.

13. If an opponent is building up on you, then try and block them with a floor.

14. Place a roof above the stairs when fighting in a house. You can edit it out if you see someone walking below.

15. If you see someone building with metal, you can hide the sound of your own construction by also using metal.▯

16. When landing in a popular zone, grab the first gun you see, then leave the second gun as bait.

17. Watch the Fortnite livestreams on Twitch.tv so you can learn tips from the professionals.

18. Campfires will still heal you even if they're underneath a ramp. This lets you snipe and heal at the same time.

19. Unfinished walls and ramps take extra damage from weapons. They are super vulnerable to explosives.

20. Wooden walls/ramps are the best because they start with the most HP when under construction.

21. Roofs/floors are sometimes better than ramps for getting a height advantage. Jump and build the tile underneath you.

22. Don't waste time emoting after a kill. It might feel good, but you're opening yourself up to being sniped.

23. Edit a wall instead of removing if you want to look outside your fort. You still get the protection of the wall.

24. Eat the mushrooms whenever possible. 5 shields doesn't sound like much, but it could save your life.

25. Taking a bit of storm damage isn't the end of the world. It can be worth it to stay inside for a bit and gather loot.

26. Don't stand near trees or boulders. They might prevent you from dropping walls or ramps.

27. Focus on mastering 2 or 3 landing zones. You'll be able to find chests faster, and grab the first gun.

28. Don't leave a trail of smashed stuff, or dropped loot behind you. You'll be tracked down and killed.

29. Once you've mastered a few spots, land in as many different areas as possible. Get a feel for the island.

30. You can jump onto a building that's too far away by jumping and building a floor tile on the side of the house.

31. Don't engage in fights if you don't have the upper hand. Focus on getting weapons, ammo, and shields.

32. Mini shields are better than bandages because everybody drops bandages when they die.

33. Chug your minis as soon as you find them. Dying with minis and having less than 50 shields is super embarrassing.

34. When playing with squads, swap out different weapons and fire them a few times to trick enemies into thinking your whole squad is nearby.

35. If you can trick enemies into thinking your whole squad is in one area, then someone can sneak around and pull an ambush maneuver.

36. Land as fast as possible at the start by aiming for rivers and lakes.

37. Include redundant tiles in bridges or towers so the whole thing doesn't collapse from one rocket attack.

38. If you find a regular shield potion and don't have any minis, chug it anyway. Don't die with shield items.

39. Focus on staying alive more than getting kills. Kills are irrelevant. You can win the game with zero kills.

40. You don't have to push every fort. Let your enemies make the mistake of trying to push *your* defensive position.

41. Damaging your own wall a few times will allow you to see through the top layer without losing protection.

42. Find a new favorite weapon if yours get nerfed. Things change. Don't be a stubborn goat.

43. Mining a fire hydrant will transform it into a jump pad. Use this to get on top of houses in the early game.

44. Learn to recognize the different noises footsteps make on different materials. This will help you know where your enemies are.

45. If your duo partner or squad buddy is under 30 hit points, knock them down and revive them back to 30.

46. Don't use doors to exit buildings. They're slow and noisy. Edit out one of your own walls or build an arch.

47. Make your opponent panic by launching explosives at his fort. Push when you think he's healing.

48. Don't engage two other players that are fighting. Wait until somebody wins, then pick off the survivor.

49. Tweak your rendering distance. This allows you to see farther, and makes sniping with the bolt-action much easier.

50. The chest noise will often go through a house's walls. So you don't always need to go inside to check it.

51. If you land a body shot with your bolt-action, swap to your AR and try to finish them off.

52. All weapons have unique firing noises. Learn the sounds they make, so you know when to push or not.

53. Don't jump from the Battle Bus and you'll land where the AFK players do. Easy way to get free pickaxe kills.

54. Trap people in the storm by hanging near the edge and sniping. One hit and the storm will finish them.

55. If you run out of mats during a fight, you need to either run or play super aggressive. No other option.

56. Spend some games farming mats and just practicing your build skills. It'll pay off in the long run.

57. When camping in your sniper tower, edit your walls to look around instead of peeking your head out.

58. Land in popular areas like Tilted Towers if you want to farm a ton of early game kills. More loot, more wins.

59. Drop a wall after blasting your shotgun if you don't have a second one. Then you can reload safely.

?

60. The farther your target, the higher above their head you need to aim if shooting with a sniper rifle.

61. If you're full of loot, you don't *need* to open every chest. You can leave some as bait for desperate players.

62. If you see two enemies fighting, kill the better one first. The better player is one dropping the most ramps/walls.

63. Better players also tend to have interesting skins/cosmetic upgrades. Remember: *Kill the pretty ones first.*

64. If your opponent stops firing at you during a fight, they're probably healing. Now's the time to push.

65. Don't heal or reload near a window or you're gonna get shot. Duck behind some furniture, or wall yourself in.

66. Try to always have at least one heal item on you. Fall, storm, or rocket damage can be unexpected.⬚

67. Taking the high ground is super important. Either learn build up quickly, or find a new game.

68. You can pick up loot faster when you've got your pickaxe out.

69. You can avoid fall damage by hugging cliffs as you fall. Also try to drop ramps.

70. The rarer a gun is, the more damage it does, in addition to being more accurate.

71. If you can't grab the loot because you're in danger, try and remember what dropped, then circle back later.

72. Always carry two shotguns so you can swap between them instead of reloading.

73. If you're in a house and you see someone building, they're probably going for the roof to headshot you.

74. Build yourself a 1x1 fort if you need to heal. If you don't, then you risk getting sniped or rocket blasted.

75. If you've got enough weapons/ammo/shields, you don't *have* to loot every enemy. Especially if it puts you in a bad spot.

76. In close combat, if your enemy has a rocket launcher, drop a wall in his face right before he fires. Boom!

77. You can't bring your resources to the next game. Use everything. Conservation is for corpses.

78. Seriously. You don't get bonus points for ending the game with a stack of unused grenades. Use them!

79. Swapping out your sniper (after landing a hit) for an AR will give you the highest possible damage output.

80. Explosives are more useful at the end of the game, when only a few people are left. Save some rockets.

81. Crouching is the quickest way to get cover when sniping over your own wall.

82. Focus fire the players who cycle through lots of different weapons. They probably have lots of mats too.⍰

83. Stay hydrated with water. Avoid energy drinks. There's more energy in an apple and a short nap than a Redbull and cup of coffee.

84. Farm your starting zone until you've got enough materials for at least two major confrontations.

85. Med-kits can be used even when you're at 80 or 90 hit points. Better to use it than lose it!

86. After you smash an enemy's wall, replace it with your own. When they investigate, edit it out and kill them.⬚

87. Chests can spawn in random fields, trucks, or the middle of nowhere. Check everything!

88. Stone and metal walls are great for protection in the end game, but build your ramps from wood.

89. Head for the roof as soon you find your first gun. Players will be running in and out of houses. Easy headshots!

90. If you see someone run into a room with no exit, throw a trap on the floor and shut the door.

91. When you run past a tree, jump, hit it twice with your pickaxe, and keep moving. Never stop moving!⁇

92. Spamming the ramp tile might save you from taking lethal fall damage when you get blown off a cliff by an impulse grenade.

93. Don't make too much noise when enemies are nearby. Even just reloading can give your position away. Crouch and become silent as death.

94. Try and avoid fights in the early game. You'll probably have a crappy weapon and take a lot of damage.

95. Don't participate in any fights when you're annoyed. Retreat and calm yourself down.

96. Stay still when sniping with non-bolt action snipers. Otherwise your bullet will never land on target.

97. Place a trap on the wall just inside a door and your opponent will never see it until it's too late.

98. Always be strafing. Never run in a straight line. Throw some jumps in there. Otherwise you'll be sniped.

⍰

99. When retreating, drop a ton of walls behind you. Your enemy will waste a lot of ammo breaking them.⍰

100. Learn all the different sounds players make when they land on things. Roofs are different than cars!

101. If you find two guns in a start zone, you can set a trap by leaving the worse one on the floor.

102. Shield items are better than healing items, because everyone drops bandages/med-kits when they die.

103. Drop a wall behind yourself if you plan on sniping someone in front of you. Don't get shot in the back.

104. If you hit someone with a boogie bomb, wait until they start jumping. They always do. Easy headshot!

105. If you're one of the last three people, avoid fighting until there are only two left. Let them spend ammo.

106. Don't drop extra healing items where enemies can easily find them. Hide those things!

107. Don't waste time looking for the enemy after you've been sniped. Run, hide, and heal!

108. Only jerks blame their squad, or duo partner for losing. Step up your game and carry!

109. Don't clutter your inventory with useless items like the bush or the port-a-fort. Focus on weapons and shields.

110. Your last enemy might not be good. Don't be afraid of them. The great players might all be dead.

111. Always aim for the head. It's the only way to guarantee a kill. You miss 100% of the headshots you don't take.

112. You'll never become a Fortnite god if you can't build properly. Spend your downtime practicing building!

113. Don't panic if you get shot. Stay calm and find your way to safety. Heal up and reengage. No panicking!

114. Activate the shoulder scope in before using your shotgun. It'll increase your damage and accuracy.

115. Don't make any unneeded noise. People who stay quiet survive the longest. Don't shoot if you won't hit.

116. When engaging enemies, pay attention to the kill feed in case they accidently kill themselves.

117. Always drop wooden walls in a firefight. They build faster and start with more health.

⍰

118. The SMG is one of the most useful weapons. Always try to keep one in your inventory.

119. One mini is not worth a second blue shotgun. Shields are not *always* better than weapons. ⍰

120. If you run into someone who's better at building, take the fight to the ground. Blow up their fort at the base.

121. Build as many walls around a panicky opponent as possible. They'll waste a lot of ammo getting free.

122. Don't build a giant fort and camp it in all game. You're just asking to get rocket swarmed.

123. Learn to use the pulse grenade. They can save you from the storm, or launch an enemy off a cliff.

124. Ramp block an enemy and they'll panic. Edit out the wall when they reload. Shoot them in the head!

125. Don't build too high or you'll take fall damage when someone collapses your tower. 3 or 4 tiles max.

126. Drop a wall on someone, and then edit a window into it. You'll surprise them and be able to shoot.

127. Don't stop and stare at the loot your enemy just dropped. Grab what you need and keep moving.

128. If you jump from the bus and aim away from the island, your parachute will deploy later, and you land faster.

129. You can shoot through most cracks and holes in your walls with the bolt-action sniper rifle.

?

130. Push your opponent when he's healing. Don't stop to heal yourself unless you're extremely low.

131. Drop a wall behind you if you're gonna pickaxe into a building. This way you won't get shot in the back.

132. Never fully mine out a tree. It will collapse and others will see it fall and will know where you are.

133. Edit out any ramps or floors you used to get yourself into a neat sniper spot. Leave no trace!

134. Master every weapon. You won't always find your favorite. Some games you'll never see a scar.

135. When looting a person who died on a lake, crouch and angle your camera skyward to see the loot.

136. Hit the blue circle when mining anything and you'll get extra resources.

137. Never fight in a house unless you're the one who's peeking *right* around the wall. Peek *left*, and die!

138. Peeking from the left side exposes too much of your body, because Fortnite models are right-handed.

139. Retreat from every fight unless you have the advantage, or you're so low on resources it doesn't matter.

140. Always snipe from a height advantage. Aim above their head. Aim beside them they're running.

141. At the start, try to go for chest spawns that come with a natural height advantage, like hills or houses.

142. Players with jump pads/bouncy pads/jetpacks can stay in the storm for longer and escape faster.

143. Build a ramp over someone's head and they might accidently crouch. Easy headshot.

144. Carry two of your favourite weapon. It's faster to swap than to reload.

145. Swapping between two shotguns lets you fire twice before your opponent reloads.

146. Avoid landing in popular areas with other players. If they find a gun before you do, then it's game over.

147. Buy a great pair of headphones. It's easier to hear the footsteps/gunfire and figure out where the enemies are.

148. Keep your eye on the total players left. Your strategies should change depending on how many are dead.

149. Minis can often be found in places like bathrooms and gas stations. Check all the nooks and crannies!

150. Change game modes if you aren't having fun. You'll never become a god if you're stressed out.

151. Use the environment as cover at the start of the game. Resources will be scarce. Play carefully.

152. Don't freak out when you die. Every loss is a learning opportunity. Just keep improving.

153. You don't need to land every last hit in order to win the game. Let your teammates get some kills.

154. Let the other players waste resources killing each other. Engage in fights only when absolutely necessary.

155. Never rage quit. Stay calm when things get bad. Try and figure out what went wrong.

156. If you feel you *must* use the bush item, don't drop it in a lake. Or on a house. Bushes don't spawn there!

157. The best sniper rifle is the bolt-action because it can kill a player with max health and shields in one hit.

158. Campfires stack. Drop a couple and your team will heal up twice as fast.

159. Loot the entire house at the start of the game. Leave nothing for the other pickaxers to pick up.

160. Use the grenade arc to throw more accurately.

161. You can wait until 14 health or so to use your med-kit/chug jug if you're trying to escape the storm.

162. Break everything in zones like Tilted to know how many mats each thing drops. Some might surprise you.

163. Wooden pallets provide an insane amount of wood. Boulders are good for stone. Cars for metal.

164. Crouching improves your accuracy while simultaneously making you harder to hit.

165. If you're falling and suspect you'll take fall damage, spam floors and maybe get lucky. Aim for buildings.

166. Use up items instead of dropping them. You don't want the enemy using them against you.

167. Shields give you a higher chance of winning the game than any other item. Try to save a spot for them.

168. Turn off the shadows in your graphics menu. This will let you spot players better. Who needs shadows anyway?

169. The closer you are to a mineable thing, the easier it is to crit it and get bonus resources.

170. Ambush an opposing squad by using one of your teammates as bait. Don't forget to revive him ;)

171. Always be friendly to random duo fills. You might form a squad someday, or learn some new tricks.

172. Clinger grenades are useful for throwing at people who open chests. Good in the early game.

173. Record your gameplay and watch it back later. Try to figure out where you went wrong. Sports pros do this.

174. Jetpacks aren't super useful at the end of the game. Ditch them for something better.

175. Damage numbers change with almost every patch. Make sure to read the notes or you'll be surprised.

176. Avoid areas like Tilted Towers if you didn't land there. It will be full of traps when you arrive.

177. Camp in map buildings more than you camp in your own tower. Camping in a tower is just asking for rockets.

178. Landing in the countryside can be safer, although you'll find less chests.

179. Ignore other players if you land in a populated area. Focus on finding a gun. Then hunt for more weapons.

180. If you're running on top of a house and you heat the chest noise, it's probably in the attic. Smash through the roof!

181. Jump pads are great for escaping the storm, but also for pushing on people you think might be healing.

182. In the final circle, toss a mini on the ground as bait. Snipe whoever comes to pick it up.

183. Wait until you have a clean shot before attempting to snipe. If you miss, then they'll drop a ton of walls.

184. Read the *entire* patch notes. Not just the parts you think concern your favorite weapons/items.

185. Keep an eye on how much health you have. Sometimes even an extra 5 shields can prevent a sniper death.

186. Use explosives on people camping in a tower. Aim for the base of the tower, and it will collapse the rest.

187. Try and get chip damage in before pushing someone. Rush in there once their shields are down.

188. Instead of taking the stairs to the basement, why not break through the floor? You might surprise someone.

189. Walls made by players are not a good source of resources. Avoid mining them. Too much noise!

190. Don't be obsessed with camping a single zone. If you're losing the fight then you need to run. Regroup.

191. Save campfires for emergency situations like when you need to snipe and heal at the same time.

192. Find some apples instead of using your med-kit. They often spawn in predictable places.

193. If you hear an explosion nearby, don't panic. Panicking is the worst thing you can do in Fortnite. (And life.)

194. Range will affect the damage for most weapons. Don't waste ammo on someone too far away.

195. You'll always get a weapon from a golden chest. Focus on finding one ASAP after jumping from the bus.

196. Keep each weapon and item in the same slot every game. Harness the power of muscle memory!

197. Ride atop your teammates rocket for a sneaky and fun way to ambush an enemy squad.

198. Spend less time mining by becoming a master at hitting that little blue circle.

199. There usually aren't any weapons, ammo, or resources left in the final circle. Plan accordingly.

200. Disengage if you're low on materials, ammo, or shields. There's no victory in being a brave idiot.

201. Drop a jump pad if you plan on camping somewhere near the final circle. Might need a quick getaway.

202. Aim for rivers/lakes after jumping from the bus. The lower the terrain, the later your chute will deploy.

203. Deploying your chute as late as possible allows you to land faster. First to land, first to find a gun. Aim away from the island to land faster.

204. Build ramps above your head when chasing someone up a cliff. Don't get shot in the head.

205. All of the houses on the map have similar layouts. Learn the layout, and master the art of house fighting.

206. If your targeting circle slows down over a bush, that means a player is hiding in that bush. (Console only.)

207. Most people don't expect to be hit by an impulse grenade. They are especially useful near cliffs.

208. If you loot someone who started in Dusty and they have no wood, that means the pallets are up for grabs.

209. Don't leave any valuable loot on the ground without covering it first. Otherwise someone else will take it.

210. Build some 1x1 forts in random spots to bait people into launching rockets, and giving away their position.

211. Winning at Fortnite is not about maximizing your kill count. That's just for people who like to show off.

212. Try to always build some walls when engaging another player. Even when sneaking from behind. You don't want to get shot from afar!

213. If you're low on health and being chased, drop a trap. The enemy will hear it, and might back off.

214. Missing with a sniper rifle will spook your target, just like hunting a deer. Go for headshots only. No body.

215. Areas near the center of the map are more likely to end up in the final circle. Get familiar with the terrain.

216. Never stop moving. If you must stop, then build yourself a 1x1 fort and be quick about it.

217. When dropping into a town, inform your teammates which building you intend to loot before you land.

218. Try and figure out a landing routine for each zone. Which building do you hit first? Where are the chests?

219. Push anyone you think is healing, regardless of their weapons and shield situation. Healers are vulnerable!

220. The weapon with the highest win-rate for solo mode victories is the bolt-action sniper rifle.

221. Spend a couple games training on every weapon/item you're uncomfortable with.

222. Apples only spawn in certain zones, and usually near trees. Mushrooms usually spawn in fields.

223. Once there are less than 10 players left, try not to engage anyone until there are 2 or 3 left.

224. Dropping a wall and attaching a ramp to it will give you double the protection.

225. At the start, don't follow players into houses thinking you'll ambush them. They might find a gun.

226. You can learn a lot by watching YouTube videos. Increase the playback speed so you can learn quicker.

227. You can shoot the balloon holding up the supply crate and it'll pop, so the crate falls quick to the ground.

228. Customize all your stuff *before* you get into the game. If you stand around tweaking stuff during a match then you might get headshot.

229. Silenced weapons are bad for close-combat, or any combat really. Use them to shoot down supply crates.

230. Drop your traps as soon as you find them if you suspect enemies are nearby. Don't die without using them.

231. Fall damage is inconsistent and sometimes begins after only two walls of height if you tumble down a cliff.

232. If you're going to camp a zone, make sure you have enough traps to defend the various access points.

233. Watch the kill feed to see which weapons the last players are using.

234. Destroying the tile under a chest will also destroy the chest. This can be useful if you have enough loot, but don't want to leave the chest.

235. The hunting rifle accuracy is affected by more things than the bolt-action. Thus, bolt is superior.

?

236. If you have a jetpack then you can build higher than your opponent, drop down, and kill his tower support tiles.

237. If following an enemy, let them open any chests. You can pick up the gun and shoot them with it.

238. Building the pyramid tile above your head is a good defensive move if you absolutely have to heal.

239. Furniture grants decent wood and only takes one hit to kill. You can smash it while hunting for chests.

240. Don't be fooled by the rarity of certain "legendary" items. Like the bush. It's not very good.

241. You can take riskier shots against players coming out of the storm because they're at less than full HP.

242. Taking and keeping the high ground is one of the most important concepts in Fortnite.

243. Most shotgun players will carry two of them, rush in after the second blast, that's when they're reloading.

244. Shooting at people too far away to kill is bad because you spook your target, and give away your position to other players in the area.

245. Adjust your mouse sensitivity until you find a balance of speed and accuracy. (Different for everyone.)

246. Make sure to have ample resources before the end phase. Often there are no materials in final circle.

247. Always fire short bursts instead of going full auto. Fire sporadically or your accuracy drops with each shot.

248. Throw grenades at players that drop into holes, or smash their way into an attic. Boom, no escape!

249. It's often the right move to drink a shield potion even when you have no shields or minis.

250. If you're always asking your squad for resources, you're either spending too much, or not mining enough.

251. If you're tower fighting at the end game, and you chip their shields off, it's a good time to push as they might try to drink a chug jug.

252. Smash all the wooden pallets at Dusty if you start there. Don't leave them for other players!

253. Never peek your head over a ledge if you can crouch and change the camera angle. It's much safer.

254. If someone is above you and shooting their way into your fort, then drop a trap on the floor, and run.

255. If someone uses a jump pad to push onto your tower, then drop and destroy your support beams.

256. If you see a tree fall on the horizon, that usually means a player mined it out, so go kill them!

257. If an enemy runs into a building, shoot the wall. The wall might collapse, and you might get another hit in.

258. If you need mats fast in a town, then jump on a roof, and mine downward. You'll mine multiple layers.

259. Always throw at least two or three grenades. The first ones will injure the enemy, third one kills.

260. Jump a split-second before you think your opponent will fire his shotgun, they will miss the headshot.

261. If you get a sniper in your first town, then head to the roof immediately. Free kills from people running around looking for weapons.

262. Try and imagine the ground is made of lava. Spend as little time as possible at ground level.

263. It's usually safe to heal in the open if you've killed a ton of people in a start zone, and everything is quiet.

264. If you're the last squadmate alive, set up a camp spot in the circle-center. Shoot players escaping the storm.

265. Always use a med-kit instead of leaving it on the ground. Even if it's just for a few health.

266. If you like to shoot from super far away, grab yourself a thermal scoped AR. Easier to find targets.

267. If you want experience killing lots of players, play a squad game without any teammates.

268. Don't be afraid to pop minis even if your shields are at 40. Especially if you're sitting on a huge stack. Better to use them, than waste them.

269. Keep track of damage numbers. You can push hard if enemies are only one shot away from death.

270. Remove all the distractions from the room. Put your cellphone on silent. Don't be distracted!

271. Don't play Fortnite when stressed. Go do something relaxing, and then come back. It's supposed to be fun!

272. Landing on the roof of a large building increases your chances of finding a chest by 50%.

273. When engaging squads, don't worry about killing knocked down players, focus on the ones still up.

274. If your teammate is knocked, block enemy shots with your body (if you have shields) to prevent him from being killed.

275. Share shield pots with teammates, even if they aren't as good as you. This helps all of you survive.

276. If you know an enemy is low, still go for a headshot. Don't get lazy and do bodyshots, because he might jump.

277. If you see enemies running out of the storm, try and wall them inside of it. They'll waste ammo breaking free.

278. Campfires are more valuable the more teammates you have.

279. If you use a bounce pad to jump on and then ride a teammate's rocket, you won't take fall damage when getting off of the rocket. (This might get bugfixed.)

280. Don't worry so much about losing. Focus on improving and it'll pay major dividends in the future.

281. When facing an enemy squad, determine who the best player is, and kill them first.

282. If you see someone running to a strange spot, they might be going to revive a teammate. Kill them both!

283. It takes more mats to take the high ground from an opponent, than to build over them in the first place.

284. If you suspect someone is in a house, build up to the roof and explore downwards.

285. You can disguise your edit pencil using the dance emote. Your opponent won't expect you to edit out the wall.

286. Be aware of which direction the bus took, and expect players to be running in from certain directions.

287. You can hack your way through a long fence almost as fast as you can walk past it. So farm that wood!

288. If pushing someone across a field, drop ramps as you move toward them. Ramps are great protection.

289. Editing a window into your wall is an easy way to kill someone. They might not even know you're there.

290. Most players jump from the bus as soon as they hit the first town. Whoever survives will have great loot.

291. Use a bounce pad to jump off a tower, then launch rockets at anybody still standing on it. No fall damage!

292. While exploring for guns, make sure to pickaxe anything that will die in one hit. Just free resources!

293. Build a tower, and drop a jump pad, then fly out a bit, and return to your tower. Great for scouting.

294. Sometimes at the start of a game you just won't find a gun, and you'll die. Shrug it off and move on. It happens.

295. C4 is useful in the early game for close combat when people don't have materials to drop protective walls.

296. If you find an apple or mushroom, then explore the area, there's like more nearby.

297. If someone builds higher than you, then put a roof on your head. Try to escape. Restart the tower race.

298. Even in a tight fight there's often time to pop a mini when your enemy reloads. Use a bandage if you can.

299. Use your bandages/medkit before you escape the storm. Someone might be waiting for you.

300. The grenade launcher is the safest gun to use to attack players without exposing yourself to return fire. Aim the arc high. Use walls for cover.

301. Since friendly rockets don't hurt teammates, you can bait an enemy by blasting a rocket at your friend's foot. They'll think he's weak.

302. While burst rifles might have better accuracy, they do less total DPS over a giant fight. Swap to one after sniping and use as a finisher.

303. Only engage with pistols when they're so close you can spit on them.

304. Shooting from too far with a pistol just spooks your enemy into hiding.

305. If you're going to ambush a squad, use an SMG because it has a large clip. If you run out of ammo you're toast. Don't be toast.

306. Focus your sniper time on the bolt and hunter rifles. Semi-autos are gross. They trick you into bad habits.

⍰

307. Get good with an AR and forget the scope mode. You can pick people off just by crouching. Way faster.

⍰

308. Don't stay in the open while reloading. AFC: Always Find Cover.

309. Watch your damage numbers. If you see low ones (like 8-9) you're not shooting efficiently. Get closer.

⁇

310. Treat a scoped AR like a sniper rifle instead of an AR. Only use it in sniper situations if you can.

311. An AR is the best weapon to grab early game. Forget the shotgun. Early close encounters are a clown fiesta.

312. When sniping, if your target is moving too much, swap to the AR. No point in wasting sniper ammo.

313. If swapping, always snipe first, then bust out the secondary. Snipers do the most damage. Use other weapons to finish them off.

314. Always take the full-auto AR over burst. Turn an auto into a burst by firing a few shots. Best of both worlds.

315. Grenade launchers are more effective in squad mode because players clump together.

316. While you can move and snipe with the hunting rifle, it's not recommended.

317. The pump is the best shotgun if you're using the Aim Down Sights function (ADS.)

318. Shotgun swapping to auto-AR has the best short-range DPS.

319. Focus on mastering 3 or 4 landing areas. If you know where all the chests spawn, you have a big advantage.

320. If someone builds above you, and you can't get the high ground, drop traps and let the enemy come to you.

321. Spray some neat patterns on a wall to distract people. They won't notice your trap on the ceiling :D

322. If you're rocking legendary guns and full shields, forget opening chests. Use them as bait for injured players.

323. Dodging rockets is easy if you never stay still. And you shouldn't be. ABM: Always Be Moving.

324. If you're having shotgun issues, you're probably not close enough. Treat it like a combat knife. Get up close and personal.

325. Chests can spawn in strange spots. Investigate every hidden nook and cranny. There's always secret loot.

326. Tap the trigger instead of holding it down. Tapping gives you better accuracy because there's more time between shots. Like burst mode.

327. If you want more trap kills then spend time in duo or squads. Knocked down players are easily trapped.

☐

328. Basic pistols suck. Don't give away your position to engage with pistols. Find a better gun.

329. Most players move in predictable ways. Watch them for a bit, then take your shot. (Especially when sniping.)

330. Quick scoping has terrible accuracy. Stabilize your reticle before firing. Calm -> Panic.

331. Rockets travel slowly. After you shoot one at someone behind a wall, take your AR and knock the wall down. Then the rocket will kill them.

332. You can improve your solo mode skills by filling in for squads. It's much tougher. Like training in heavy gravity.

333. Drop your mouse sensitivity if you prefer using the AR. Makes it easier to land shots.

334. The heavy shotgun has the best DPS output of its class if you're skilled. Can take some practice though.

335. Bait in your opponent by using a pistol. He'll think you don't have a better weapon. When they get close, swap to your shotgun.

336. Always crouch before shooting, even if you have height advantage.

337. Drop traps on your enemy's path if they're running through the same area a lot. They'll think it's safe since they've been there before.

338. In shotgun battles the High ground is very important. Ramp rush the enemy and get above them.

339. Use an obvious trap to funnel someone down a passage where you've hidden other traps.

340. Use third-person view to scope around corners. Safer than sticking your head out.

341. Pistols should only be used at the start of the game. It's a beginner weapon, don't master them.

342. You might find it easier to lead shots if you tweak the ADS settings.

343. The artificial delay makes it faster to switch from shotguns to another weapon than vice versa.

344. Sniping is the only way to get better at sniping. Spend a few games doing this exclusively.

345. Hiding beside objects like cars, boulders, and trees will prevent most rocket damage.

⍰

346. If you like to jump and shoot you should use a pistol. Its accuracy isn't diminished by movement.

347. If using an auto AR, aim for the head at first, then switch to body once the firing bloom expands.

348. Get an enemy to chase you by emptying a clip and not reloading. They'll think you're out of ammo.

349. Pistols are *somewhat* useful as a cleanup weapon in the mid-game. But really you should ditch them ASAP. Any healing item is better than a pistol.

350. Pistol DPS will display as higher than grey ARs, but they're only good for short range.

351. If forced to use a pistol, you *have* to aim for the head. It's the only way to out DPS your enemy. Play to win!

352. Landing in the forest is safer, but you have less chance of winning the game since there's less loot.

353. When unloading at close range, a suppressed pistol will do more damage than a suppressed SMG.

354. You have to ditch your fort if under siege from multiple angles. The fort is a sunk cost. Don't die because you don't want to "waste mats."

355. The rarity of a gun doesn't mean that it's better. Don't be a slave to a better color. Think for yourself.

356. Use your traps when fighting inside. Don't save them for the next fight. There might not be one.

357. Try to always snipe from roughly the same distance so you can get used to how much the bullet drops.

358. Pistols rarely get kills at long range. You're giving away your position for nothing. Find a new weapon!

359. SMGs/ARs are better for fighting multiple enemies, while shotguns are better for a single enemy.

360. The only weapon that is usually the best for any range or situation is the golden SCAR. It's a remarkable exception to most rules.

371. To maximize damage on a structure, use a grenade launcher. You might have to practice your angles or you'll get bad bounces.

372. Avoid scope mode if you're on the console. Use the auto-aim. It's really really good. Especially for ARs.

373. High-damage slow-firing pistols should be treated like shotguns with slightly better range.

374. Since you can't get crits with rockets or grenades, aim for the feet to maximize splash damage.

375. The best time to engage with pistols is against an enemy with a shotgun. If they miss, you'll have to kill them with a few headshots.

376. Want trap kills? Ride the bus all the way to the end. You'll parachute out with all the other AFKs.

377. Keep the cursor at chest height if you're waiting for someone to step through a door. Then go full auto.

378. Crouching with an AR can turn it into a sort of sniper rifle. Use burst.

379. Crouching with an SCAR won't increase your hit chance that much. Treat it like a sort of sniper rifle. Go for long distance standing shots.

380. If someone is building up, and you don't want to waste good ammo, unload your pistol for chip damage.

381. Always hide when reloading with a sniper. It takes long and if you stay in the open you'll get shot for no reason.

382. It's normal to lose at the start. It will take you hundreds of games to hone your skills. Stay calm!

383. Understand that in games it's possible to make the correct move and still lose due to luck. Just move on and stay focused on winning.

384. While you shouldn't master them, pistols are plentiful at the start of the game. So get at least good with them.

385. If you suck at headshots then grab and SMG and aim for the neck. The bloom will net you some head shots.

⍰

386. Full auto should only be used in a few situations. Like killing walls. Otherwise go burst mode.

387. Pistol rarity doesn't mean much. Don't put yourself in a bad spot to grab an upgrade. Skill matters more.

388. With a sniper and SMG you don't need an AR. Adapting your playstyle to your current items is critical to victory.

389. Search for chests in places with higher elevation. Hills, tall buildings, etc. Find a weapon, and you'll have height advantage, so more headshots.

390. When sniping at an enemy squad, focus on the best player. They'll be moving the most, have the best skin.

391. If you have nasty ammo, use it to knock down walls. Save the heavy ammo for PvP encounters.

392. Rarity has a big impact on ARs. Ditch your current AR if you find a color upgrade, even if you aren't great with that weapon. You must learn!

393. If you can master angles and bounces, then the grenade launcher is the ultimate sieging weapon.

394. Stay still when shooting your AR and you're gonna get splattered and have a rotten day.

395. Pistols are designed to be bad. They have random bullet spray/bloom. Don't spend a lot of time with them.

396. SMG damage at long distance is total garbage. Accuracy is also horrible. Better to sneak in close and then blast.

397. Bullets are affected by gravity in Fortnite more than in other games. Takes some getting used to.

398. Aiming down the sights is not great for close combat. You lose too much maneuverability. Save it for medium range.

399. If you miss the kill after aiming for the head, then switch to body shots. The enemy will be spooked and moving too much for head shots.

400. If doing a two shotgun swap combo, start with pump, and then swap to tactical. Two pumps will give you a bigger delay. Not worth it.

401. As accuracy drops with each shot, you should switch to feet/body with an SMG after firing for a few seconds.

401. SMGs use an insane amount of ammo. Hoard it like pirate gold!

402. A chug jug isn't great bait because nobody in their right mind would leave that on the ground. Minis however...

403. In squads, try to get at least 2 rocket launchers. Then you can rocket spam an enemy fort. First rocket kills the wall, second kills the players.

404. Shooting a minigun from the passenger's seat in a shopping cart will propel you faster than the battle bus.

405. It takes multiple headshots to kill someone with a pistol. So don't go being a hero with it. It's tougher.

406. If you build a 1x1 fort in the middle of nowhere, the enemy might think you're healing. They'll attack it, and give away their position.

407. While sniping, if you're hitting the wall instead of the head, then you're aiming too low. Compensate for bullet drop and aim higher.

408. Want trap kills? Land in Tilted Towers. Drop traps inside the doorway of larger buildings.

409. Hand cannon = sniper rifle with medium range instead of long.

410. Hand cannons can be used at longer ranges. You can treat them like bad sniper rifles with medium range.

411. Don't be too cautious when sniping. Line up a good shot and go for it. Perfect opportunities rarely occur.

412. You don't need to check inside small houses/trucks for chests. If you don't hear the noise, move on.

413. With a shotgun you must wait for the perfect opportunity. You might only get one shot off for a fight. Don't waste it, or you'll get splattered.

414. If the target is moving, consider sniping for the body. Moving head shots are extremely difficult.

415. The grenade launcher is bad at close range. Bad bounces can ruin your day. Use it as a siege weapon.

416. Land on the roof of a house instead of going in the front door. This way you'll get to the attic chest before anybody else gets there.

417. Don't break any walls you don't have to. It makes noise and you're just destroying your own cover.

418. It's safer to fire from an uncovered spot in the early stages because players are hunting for chests.

419. If you hear someone in your house, head for the roof. If you can't find him, he might be in the basement. Maybe shielding up. Go get him!

420. Balloons are basically useless. Keep them until you find literally anything else. Then swap them out.

421. If you're stressed then take a break. Go for a walk! A 30 minute walk can improve your cognitive abilities.

422. If you can't tell where your enemy is, then box yourself in until you get a read on his position. Play safe!

423. Footsteps make a very distinct sound on dirt and stone. Makes it easier to tell if someone is inside the house or outside/beneath.

424. The aggressive pusher is usually the winner. It's all about playing to win instead of playing to not lose.

425. Treat each enemy like a pro. Never underestimate them, or you might take unnecessary damage.

426. Secret passageways are great for free building mats. You can make lots noise and not attract attention.

427. If you know which direction the bus took, then you'll know where the majority of players will be coming into the circle from. Ambush them!

428. Mounted turrets are great when you know there's only one enemy around. Otherwise you're vulnerable.

429. If being pushed by a grappler, swap to an AR and unload. Don't let them close the distance for free.

430. There are some structures you can't build off of (like curved roofs.) Know which is which and you'll have an advantage in build wars.

431. Boxing yourself in a 1x1 isn't trapping yourself. You must learn to edit in windows. Then it's like you built yourself a pillbox.

432. Running out of the storm is a great time to pop a slurp. You could exit with more HP/shields!

433. Four weapons and one shield or healing item is the ideal inventory.

434. Before entering a new town, scout around the edges for people eating apples/mushrooms.

435. If you see the remnants of a build fight, there are probably some good players in the area.

436. If under pressure, wall up until your enemy reloads, then pop your healing items.

437. If someone drops a turret on their building, drop underneath it. They can't fire down.

438. If fighting someone and a third person shows up, make sure you don't end as up the man in the middle. Move so another enemy is the middle target.

439. If you see two players fighting, that's a great time to drop a turret. (Make sure to set up defensive walls.)

440. Better to pop a chug jug for 5 shields than to leave it on the ground for someone else.

441. If you build alongside your enemy's tower you can take advantage of his ramps. Free housing, yo.

442. People camping on top of hills are usually afraid of close combat. Be aggressive and push them.

443. Push with pyramids against someone using a rocket launcher. You can prevent most of the damage.

444. Turrets make your floors harder to break (1,000 HP.) So you can drop them defensively without using them.

445. You'll know immediately after landing on a roof if there's a chest underneath you. No chest? Move on.

446. When you first land, other players might go for the same chest as you just opened. Let them break the wall down, and you wait for them with the gun.

447. If the enemy has a shotgun, drop a wall, after they shoot it edit out the wall. It will surprise your enemy, as they expected to shoot the wall again.

448. Don't engage unless you have enough ammo to secure a kill.

449. If you hear someone drinking a shield, then push hard. They're locked down for at least a few seconds.

450. If you find a big shield at the start, drink it anyway. Don't wait for minis, or you might end up dead.

451. If you totally miss your first few bursts, consider retreating. You've lost the first strike advantage.

452. If you hear someone pumping balloons, then wait until they start floating up to engage.

453. If you only have one shotgun, instead of swapping, build between the shots. Defends while you reload.

454. Approach a new town from height advantage so you can scope out the houses. Visit any that look untouched. Could be some chests left in there.

455. If you know the enemy is weak you can be a lot more aggressive. Dive in there if he's one shot from death.

456. Build your fort near a rift so you can evacuate ASAP if there's trouble.

457. Sometimes it's okay to just wait on a hill. Build a minor fort and let the enemy come to you. Running around looking for people can be dangerous.

458. Keep an eye on your ammo. If you're down to your last 10 AR shots you might want to bail. We often use more ammo than we think we need.

459. When landing with the glider, spam jump as you hit the ground. You'll get a minor kick called a bunny hop. Makes you harder to hit.

460. Watch the kill feed for trap kills. Their loot might be just sitting there for someone to come grab.

461. A good sign a building hasn't been looted is if there's ammo on the roof.

462. At the start always wall yourself in before opening a chest. If you heard the noise, someone else heard it too.

463. Always push someone you think just won a fight. Odds are they're weak and low on ammo/mats.

464. If your enemy's shots fewer and far between, they're probably running low on ammo. Push them hard!

465. Make sure there aren't any traps before barging into your dead enemy's fort to collect his loot.

466. Swap to another weapon to dump all your balloons at once.

467. When landing on someone's 1x1, land on the edge. If they build a wall or ramp, you'll spawn atop the wall. Also, you can't get trap killed.

468. If you land right next to someone with a rocket launcher they might just suicide and kill you both. Be careful.

469. Based on the circle and initial bus direction, you should be able to tell where the majority of players are. Avoid this area until late.

470. When engaging at close range, you can always just build walls until your enemy runs low on ammo. Then you can start shooting. No rush!

471. Keep your rocket launcher hidden as long as possible. Enemies will play differently if they know you have it.

472. If your enemy is in your tower and gets stuck, like by a ramp, that's a perfect opportunity to trap kill him.

473. Sitting for too long is bad. Get up and walk around every so often or you'll look like an old man by 25.

474. If you lose track of an enemy, box yourself in and edit the walls. Look around and find them while protected.

475. Build a ramp before you hit the ground to take less fall damage. Try to land higher up on the ramp.

476. Build a ramp with a roof on top of it and you might take zero fall damage. (Or at least greatly reduced damage.)

477. Panic is all in your head. Staying calm under pressure is one of the most important Fortnite skills.

478. It's okay to knock down trees and make lots of noise at the start. Players are occupied looking for weapons.

479. After getting your first gun, focus on killing nearby players. They might not have shields yet. Kill them fast so you get the rest of the loot.

480. Once you get good you should land in the bigger cities. There's more enemies, but lots more loot. More loot equals higher chance of winning.

481. Don't get into crazy build wars at the start. Save the mats for later.

482. Don't panic when you see an enemy with better weapons. This game is 90% skill, and 10% loot.

483. Be efficient with mats at the start of the game. Don't blow 300 wood on a single fight. You might be fighting a noob. No point in spending resources.

484. You can use the roof of a golf cart as a jump pad. Spam walls as you jump and you'll get a quick 3-story tower.

485. Build a pyramid on the roof of your 1x1 if you want to edit peek and check out your surroundings.

486. Loot lake can be crossed for only 120 wood instead of 240 if you build ramps and jump off the top of them, then jump again as you hit the ground.

487. Knocked players can be evacuated faster if you drop a bounce pad on a backwards ramp.

488. Drop an edited pyramid onto a spike trap and you won't take any damage when it goes off.

489. If an enemy is building up on you, drop a pyramid onto his ramp and it'll jam him from building.

490. The best way to counter an enemy's pyramid is to blow it up with an SMG or heavy sniper.

491. A fast way to get down from a tower is to fall, build two walls and a ramp, and repeat until you hit ground.

492. Use auto run and to sort your inventory/drop ammo for a teammate. Yes you'll be running in a straight line, but it's better than standing still!

493. Dropping a rotated ramp toward your enemy and running in a straight line is the safest way to escape a field.

494. To reload a shotgun without slowing down, jump, reload one bullet, and swap guns. Keep moving, swapping, and jumping. Never stop!

495. To build a ramp tower, start with a pyramid, attach a ramp to it, and build vertically while jumping.

496. If a tile won't let you place a floor on it, it might let you put a pyramid.

497. If using C4 on someone holed up in a 1v1, throw two charges. They detonate a fraction of a second after each other, and one hurts the player.

498. For a great push tactic, jump, spin 180°, drop a ramp and jump pad, and take off. Gets you there super fast.

499. Destroy your launch pads without using ammo by editing the attached ramp into a floor, but not confirming the edit until after you jump off.

500. Place a wall at the top edge of a hill. Attach a spike trap to it then hide it with a ramp. Presto, invisible trap!

501. If you bounce off the top of a tree you might not take fall damage.

502. If someone boxes you in and puts a spike trap, run to the opposite wall. You might not take any damage!

503. You can kill a freshly placed spike trap before it goes off by hitting it twice with your pickaxe.

504. Passengers in vehicles can use emotes. This makes you harder to hit.

505. If someone runes into a room, drop a ramp at the door, then toss a grenade in. They can't run out.

506. Add a pyramid on top of your double ramp to prevent someone with a minigun from ruining your day.

507. Instead of dropping down to shotgun someone, jump -> shoot -> build a floor. This way you get headshots, but no risk of fall damage.

508. It's faster to build up high by going ramp -> pyramid -> jump ->ramp, than ramp -> ramp -> ramp.

509. If someone runs into a room, throw a clinger on the door, then open the door. They'll run out and BOOM!

510. If you see two people in a build fight, use a heavy sniper to knock the support ramps from their towers. You can get two kills with zero risk.

511. Bounce pads, walls, and floors are the quickest way to build high. You'll need lots of pads though. Pad, bounce -> wall, wall, wall, floor –> repeat

512. Dropping onto a golf cart will prevent fall damage because the tops act like a bounce pad.

513. You can place a pyramid through a pre-built house floor/roof.

514. If you use your pickaxe on an enemy's fort and they're three tiles above you, they won't hear you. Use this to knock out their support tiles.

515. Throw a clinger at a wall, then shoot down the wall, and the clinger will explode, hurting the player.

516. In duos, snipe in teams. One with a heavy sniper to knock down walls, and one to headshot the enemy.

517. Hitting only 20% of your sniper shots would be amazing. Don't worry about missing. Missing is fine.

518. Double-ramp double-floor pushing is safest against spammy weapons like high damage SMGs.

519. Editing and rebuilding a steel wall allows you to look through it and scout out what the enemies are up to.

520. Peak through the holes in your 1x1 with a thermal AR to spy on enemy players.

521. To stop someone from holing in a 1x1, smash their wall twice with your pickaxe, and replace their wall with one of your own.

522. Crouching while falling is great. Land on the edge of the ramp you're spamming. No fall damage!

523. With recent updates to the rocket launcher, it's now possible to ride your own rocket. Shoot down, jump, ride!

524. When using edits to scout what players are doing, use ramps instead of walls. Walls are opaque now!

525. If you escape your town with a bounce pad, shoot the pad as you float away. Then the enemy can't use it. Then you can blow up the tower, GG!

526. Rift diving on to someone's head causes their builds to appear behind you. Impossible to counter.

527. To juggle a sixth item and bring it with you, run forward, look up, and spam the item interact key.

528. If you jump from a tower in a build fight, build a new mini tower so you'll have height advantage if your opponent also jumps.

529. Strafe from side to side when pushing up someone with ramps. Makes you harder to hit!

530. Take advantage of muscle memory. Drop your traps each game and pick them up in the same order so your loadout is constant.

531. If you can drop a floor and a launch pad before you hit the ground (very hard) you'll take no fall damage.

532. Brick and metal start with more relative HP now, so wood isn't always the best option. Still the fastest!

533. Improving your skills in various parts of the game (building, sniping, etc) is more important than winning.

534. A spiral staircase hut is the best 1x1 to snipe from because the stairs will take damage before your face.

535. You can snipe from the tiny gaps in a pyramid + edited window. (Only snipers can shoot from these gaps.)

536. Learn where all the portals and rifts go to have a map advantage over your opponents.

537. Place traps above/next to portals to take out annoying map jumpers.

538. You can hear your traps trigger from far away. Use these as a type of motion sensor.

539. Set up traps in the bottom of bunkers to catch unwary players as they drop down to what they think is safety. But no. Blamo. They're toast.

540. Turrets throw off the auto targeting reticle. If you weave between turrets you'll be harder to hit.

541. Swap from deagle to heavy sniper to kill a wall, and then the player.

542. If someone is spamming walls in your face, drop a ramp behind you and jump as they place the wall. You'll phase through their wall.

543. Always carry a weapon that can one-shot a wall if you like build battles. Don't get boxed in!

544. You can kill a trap through a door by using your pickaxe. Hit the trap once, close the door. The crit circle remains in the same place.

545. Don't give up even if you lose a lot of games. Focus on improving!

546. All the best players started out as noobs. It's natural to want to quit. But winners don't quit. They soldier on.

547. To hide in a house, find a room with two nearby doors. Open them both and stand in the corner.

548. You can run faster with a balloon. Run, jump, run, jump. You're easier to hit, but travel faster in a straight line.

549. If you were a fan of the glider redeploy, then you might want to grab a stack of balloons even though they're mostly useless and should die.

550. Balloons can be used by the passenger in vehicles to levitate your quad crasher. Float away. Have fun!

551. Quad crashers don't take damage when crashing. So go nuts. Pretend you're Superman. You basically are.

552. Trigger an ice trap to travel fast across an area. Great for escaping.

553. Since you can heal while sliding, it's not the end of the world to get ice trapped. Just pop your bandages and peace out.

554. Balloon running + ice trap = mega fast Olympic gold medalist levels of sprinting. (Very fast.)

555. Drop a campfire before trying to resurrect a knocked down noob.

556. Weapons that pop from chests appear on the right of the chest. So if you and another player are racing for the same chest, stand on the right!

557. Build speed can be tweaked in your settings. Check it out!

558. If playing on the console, swap your edit button to a d-pad. Makes it much quicker.

559. Reading the patch notes every patch is super important. So many things change you'd be a donkey not check it out.

560. Drop multiple campfires around your tower if in the final circle. Never know when you'll drop down.

561. Campfires prevent lethal damage and leave you with 1 HP, if you're lucky.

562. Boogie bombs will stop working if you do even a single point of damage to the enemy. So aim for the head.

563. Pump shotguns can't be found in chests (currently.) So stop looking!

564. If you have your weapon out, you can see if a tree has been smacked or not. Pickaxe doesn't show this unless you're close enough to hit the tree.

565. Three loot llamas will spawn each game. So keep your eye out.

566. Pads can be dropped on ramps. Not just floors. Ramps! Imagine that.

567. The bigger the rock, the less stone it gives you when you kerblamo it with your pickaxe. Why is that? Who cares. Stick to small rocks!

568. If someone is chasing you, build some ramps, then a floor, and drop a trap on the floor. Then more ramps. They'll chase you, and die!

567. Always build a floor once you create a port-a-fort. This way other players can't use it.

568. If you shoot a rocket through a window at close range, they'll take damage, but you won't.

569. If you've got more than 2 traps, leave some as you go. Random traps often give you kills because enemies don't expect them.

570. Swap quickly between two bolt actions and you can stay zoomed in.

571. If a map hut has crack/hole in it, you can probably snipe through it.

572. Smashing a llama with your pickaxe is the quickest way to pop it.

573. You can warm up the mini gun while falling. Better than busting it out when you hit the floor and see the enemy with a shotgun and you're like, "Oh boy, now I'm toast."

574. While you should leave up large trees, you can fully kill small trees without giving away your position.

575. If thrown in the right place, C4 can blow up an entire house. Get good with it and become a Kaboom Wizard.

576. Jump from the bus ASAP and aim toward the ocean and you'll hit the ground before other players.

577. Once you jump from the bus, you can glide anywhere you want. You aren't limited to close places.

578. Pawn shops in Tilted Towers have hidden basements. You might find a few chests down there.

579. If you hear the chest noise and aren't near a building/truck, it might be in a sewer under your feet.

580. If you find an airdrop or llama, wall it in before looting it. Otherwise you might get sniped.

581. It takes half a second to build a 1x1. So don't be lazy. Never heal in the open. Don't expose your head.

582. Landing in popular zones with lots of players is the best way to improve. If you always land in fields you'll never get that sweet PvP experience.

583. Hold down your build key to activate turbo building. This lets you build mega fast. Too fast really.

584. If you have to walk through water (not recommended) then at least jump through it. You'll go much faster!

585. If someone with a default skin starts building as soon as you shoot them, it might be a pro in disguise.

586. Hop rocks last for 30 seconds. Plenty of time to push someone camping out in their stupid fort.

587. Build a roof on top of your stairs and you'll double up the hit points.

588. The SCAR has the best first shot accuracy because the timer resets faster than other guns.

589. Never emote after killing someone unless it's the last player in the game. But still... Bad manners!

590. Editing players are vulnerable. You'll be able to get the first shot off. Use a shotgun. Make it count!

591. If you land on tires you won't take fall damage (from any height.)

592. Reset the ramp tile after you're done fighting. Otherwise you might be in for a surprise next engagement.

593. Reinventing the wheel is a dumb idea. For the best keybinding setups, copy a pro player.

594. Ramps built up a mountain won't collapse if the bottom tile is shot out.

595. If sniping on a ramp, build walls on both sides. Not just the side you think is so so so dangerous.

596. Editing downward is easier than other directions. Great way to practice being an edit star.

597. Wait for first shot accuracy to kick in before firing your gun. Reset it if you aren't confident of the distance.

598. You don't have to build a giant fort every fight. Especially at the start. Save your mats and play smarter.

599. While running and jumping forward, scan to your left and right (doesn't slow you down.) More information is just better!

600. This is the 600th tip. So it better be a good one, right? Okay here we go: **Be the teammate you want to see in the world.** Lead by example. Never be mean to other players, especially friends. Getting angry doesn't increase your win chance. It lowers it. So stay frosty and stay awesome. Have a great day. Thanks for reading.

Made in the USA
Columbia, SC
09 December 2018